D0623107

Do You Really Want a Guinea Pig?

Bridget Heos • Illustrated by Katya Longhi

Amicus Illustrated is published by Amicus
P.O. Box 1329, Mankato, MN 56002
www.amicuspublishing.us

Library of Congress Cataloging-in-Publication Data
Heos, Bridget, author.
  Do you really want a guinea pig? / by Bridget Heos ;
illustrated by Katya Longhi.
    pages cm. — (Amicus illustrated) (Do you really want a pet?)
  Summary: "A mischievous guinea pig (and the narrator) teach a young boy
the responsibility—and the joys—of caring for a pet guinea pig. Includes 'Is this
pet right for me?' quiz"— Provided by publisher.
  Audience: K to grade 3.
  Includes bibliographical references.
  ISBN 978-1-60753-749-6 (library binding) — ISBN 978-1-60753-848-6 (ebook)
  1. Guinea pigs as pets–Juvenile literature. 2. Pets–Juvenile literature. I. Longhi,
Katya, illustrator. II. Title. III. Series: Heos, Bridget. Do you really want a pet?
  SF459.G9H43 2016
  636.935'92–dc23   2014033270

Editor   Rebecca Glaser
Designer   Kathleen Petelinsek

Printed in the United States of America at
Corporate Graphics in North Mankato, Minnesota.

10 9 8 7 6 5 4 3 2 1

About the Author

Bridget Heos is the author of more than
70 books for children including *Mustache Baby*
and *Mustache Baby Meets His Match*. Her family
has two pets, an old dog named Ben and a young
cat named Homer. You can find out more about
her at www.authorbridgetheos.com.

About the Illustrator

Katya Longhi was born in southern Italy.
She studied illustration at the Nemo NT
Academy of Digital Arts in Florence. She loves
to create dream worlds with horses, flying
dogs, and princesses in her illustrations.
She currently lives in northern Italy
with her Prince Charming.

So you say you want a guinea pig. You really, really want a guinea pig. **But do you *really* want a guinea pig?**

Your guinea pig will need a home.

Not just *your*
home, but a cage.

4

The cage will need soft bedding, a box for sleeping and hiding, a water bottle, and most important: a food bowl! You'll need to feed your guinea pig twice a day.

FOOD

If you don't…

. . . he'll complain, with loud squeaks. After all, he's hungry. And eating is a guinea pig's favorite pastime!

I'm starving!

Feed your guinea pig hay, guinea pig pellets, and vegetables. But don't give him potatoes, onions, or iceberg lettuce. Those will give him a tummy ache.

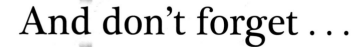

And don't forget . . .

... treats! Fruit is nature's candy, especially to guinea pigs.

Could I see the dessert menu, please?

Feeding a guinea pig is fun.

DESSERT MENU

APPLES

BANANAS

STRAWBERRIES

MELONS

ORANGES

Cleaning a cage is less fun.
But it must be done!
If it's not...

9

... the cage will become a guinea *pig sty*!
And that could make your guinea pig sick.

Clean out everything inside the cage. Put in new bedding. Now that you've taken care of the basics, you'll need to tame your guinea pig. **If you don't…**

... he'll be afraid. And he won't come out to play.

Let's play hide—but not seek.

To tame your guinea pig, first sit next to his cage and talk to him.

Once upon a time there was a boy who loved his guinea pig.

Feed him a small piece of carrot from your hand, then pet his head. After several days, your guinea pig will trust you.

Now, you can carefully pick him up. Sit on the floor and hold him with two hands against your chest.

This is a good time to brush your guinea pig.
If he has long hair, brush him every day.

If you don't . . .

. . . his hair will be a tangled mess! Plus guinea pigs like being brushed. It's relaxing.

Worst hair day ever!

16

While you brush your guinea pig, make sure he's healthy. If you see crusty eyes or drooling, or if he stops eating, take him to the vet.

When your guinea pig is feeling better, you can play together. Your guinea pig might like to play with a little ball or even play outside.

Keep him in an enclosed area. Otherwise your guinea pig might run away. He won't go far. But he may be hard to find. Maybe he really is playing hide and seek!

Guinea pigs
really are sweet.

Found you!

So if you're willing to house,
feed, water, groom, play with, and
protect your new pet, maybe you
really do want a guinea pig.

Now I have a question for the guinea pig.

You say you want a person.
You really, really want a person.

But do you *really*
want a person?

Of course you do!

Good guinea pig, Furry.

Good person, J.J.!

QUIZ

Is this the right pet for me?

Should you get a guinea pig? Take this quiz to find out. (Be sure to talk to breeders, rescue groups, or pet store workers, too!)

1. Do you have a spot in your living room or other family gathering area for a cage?
2. Do you have the time and patience to tame an animal?
3. Can you be calm and careful with a small animal?
4. Can you live with the squeaks and chatter of an animal that is noisy at times?

If you answered . . .

a. NO TO ONE, a hamster might be a better fit. Guinea pigs crave interaction with people. Hamsters prefer a quieter environment.
b. NO TO TWO, an animal that stays in its cage, such as a finch, may be better.
c. NO TO THREE, you may like a larger animal, such as a cat or dog.
d. NO TO FOUR, a quieter animal, such as a rabbit or snake might be a better fit.
e. YES TO ALL FOUR QUESTIONS, a guinea pig might be the right pet for you!

23

Websites

Guinea Pig Care | AAHA
www.aaha.org/pet_owner/pet_health_library/other/
general_health/guinea_pig_care.aspx
This site, sponsored by the American Animal Hospital
Association, features tips on how to care for guinea pigs.

Guinea Pigs: The Humane Society of the United States
www.humanesociety.org/animals/guinea_pigs/
The Humane Society has advice on bringing a new
guinea pig home, feeding, and housing.

Interesting Facts about Guinea Pigs: Fitzroy Vet Hospital
fitzroyvet.com.au/pet-library/interesting-facts-about-
guinea-pigs
Read about different names for guinea pigs, how long
they live, and more!

It's My Life: Why We Have Pets | PBS Kids Go
pbskids.org/itsmylife/family/pets/
Read about the joys and responsibilities of adding a pet
to your family, with firsthand accounts from other kids
who own pets.

Every effort has been made to ensure that these websites are appropriate
for children. However, because of the nature of the Internet, it is impossible
to guarantee that these sites will remain active indefinitely or that their
contents will not be altered.

Read More

Bearce, Stephanie. *Care for a Pet
Guinea Pig*. How to Convince Your
Parents You Can— Hockessin, Del.:
Mitchell Lane Publishers, 2010.

Carr, Aaron. *Guinea Pig*. I Love My
Pet. New York: AV2 by Weigl, 2013.

Johnson, Jinny. *Guinea Pigs*. My New
Pet. Mankato, Minn.: Smart Apple
Media, 2014.

Niven, Felicia Lowenstein. *Learning to
Care for Small Mammals*. Beginning
Pet Care with the American Humane
Society. Berkeley Heights, N.J.: Bailey
Books, 2011.

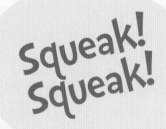

Squeak!
Squeak!

24